THE
VICTORIAN
ASYLUM

Sarah Rutherford

SHIRE PUBLICATIONS

Published in Great Britain in 2010 by Shire Publications
Ltd, Midland House, West Way, Botley, Oxford OX2 0PH,
United Kingdom.
44-02 23rd Street, Suite 219, Long Island City, NY 11101,
USA.
E-mail: shire@shirebooks.co.uk · www.shirebooks.co.uk

© 2008 Sarah Rutherford. First published 2008; reprinted
2010.

Every attempt has been made by the publisher to secure
the appropriate permissions for materials reproduced in
this book. If there has been any oversight we will be happy
to rectify the situation and a written submission should be
made to the Publishers.

A CIP catalog record for this book is available from the
British Library.

Shire Library no. 461 • ISBN-13:978 0 74780 669 1

Sarah Rutherford has asserted her right under the
Copyright, Designs and Patents Act, 1988,
to be identified as the author of this book.

Designed by Ken Vail Graphic Design, Cambridge, UK and
typeset in Perpetua and Gill Sans.
Printed in China through Worldprint Ltd.

10 11 12 13 14   10 9 8 7 6 5 4 3 2

COVER IMAGE
Buckinghamshire County Asylum, Stone, a small rural
county asylum (built 1850–3).

TITLE PAGE IMAGE
James Hadfield (1771–1841) tried to assassinate King
George III in 1800 and became a patient at Bethlem until
his death. He kept pet animals and birds in his cell,
including cats, dogs and a squirrel, and wrote, illustrated
and sold poems. This epitaph to his 'Poor Jack, squirrel'
also shows his caged canaries. (© Bethlem Art and History
Collections Trust.)

CONTENTS PAGE IMAGE
The women's airing court at Broadmoor (see page
39).

ACKNOWLEDGEMENTS
Many people have patiently advised and supported me in the
preparation of this book. I wish particularly to thank those
who encouraged and advised me, including my sister, Cathy
Glean, my tutor and friend Judith Shaw (formerly Roberts),
and my friends Marion Wickham and Nigel Halse. Many
archivists have been extremely helpful, particularly Julian
Pooley of Surrey History Centre, Michael Phillips of Bethlem
Royal Hospital Archives and Museum, and Morag Williams,
archivist of the Crichton Royal Hospital, Dumfries.

Illustrations are acknowledged as follows: Reproduced
by permission of Dumfries and Galloway Health Board,
pages 7 (top), 46 (bottom); Reproduced by permission of
East Sussex Archives, pages 6 (top), 44 (bottom); Cadbury
Lamb, pages 13 (bottom), 16; The Lightbox Museum,
Woking, pages 32 (bottom), 34 (top), 38 (top), 43 (top);
Reproduced by permission of City Of London, London
Metropolitan Archives, page 21 (bottom); Reproduced by
permission of Somerset Record Office, page 12 (bottom);
Reproduced by permission of Surrey History Centre (©
Surrey History Centre), pages 6 (bottom), 22, 28, 31 (top),
32 (top), 35 (bottom), 36, 37 (top), 39 (bottom), 41 (left), 42, 43 (bottom), 44 (top), 45 (both); Reproduced by
permission of Teesside Archives, page 33; Reproduced by
permission of Comer Homes, page 50.
Other illustrations are taken from contemporary
publications, the source being identified in the caption, or
are photographs by the author.

Shire Publications is supporting the Woodland Trust, the UK's leading
woodland conservation charity, by funding the dedication of trees.

CONTENTS

Queen Elizabeth

The Duke of York

A Thorn between two Roses

The Queen of Hearts

Captain Cuff

The Comic Element

Fine feathers

Well flowers

Mother Goose

AN M.C.

TEMPLE BAR

She wore a wreath of Roses

QUESTION MEETING OF THE EMPERORS

WAR

COMMUNICATION CUT OFF

LATEST

ZULU

COURT END OF THE TRIAL

NOTICE

SPECIAL EDITION

WAR NEWS

The latest Editions !!!

A Keeper

An Obstruction

The Ruling Spirit

For this night only

INTRODUCTION

Vᴦ ᴵˢᴵᴛᴵⁿᴳ a lunatic asylum is not a pleasant idea for most people. Various emotions might be aroused: distaste, because of stories of people needlessly incarcerated and badly treated; uneasiness, or fear of the unknown, because these isolated institutions were so effective at restricting visitors. Although the Victorian asylum had a forbidding reputation, and asylums had their failings, they were constructed as benevolent and compassionate facilities for vulnerable people.

Defined as 'an institution for the shelter and support of afflicted or destitute persons, in particular, for the insane', the asylum was one of many institutions developed as essential parts of Victorian society, along with workhouses, prisons, hospitals, boarding schools, public parks and cemeteries.

Asylum estates had an unlikely model, the country house estate. W. A. F. Browne, Superintendent of the Montrose Royal Lunatic Asylum, in his book *What Asylums Were, Are and Ought to Be* (1837), enthused about the similarities between the palace for the mad and the palace for the aristocrat:

'Conceive a spacious building resembling the palace of a peer, airy, and elevated, and elegant, surrounded by extensive and swelling grounds and gardens... The sun and air are allowed to enter at every window, the view of the shrubberies and fields, and groups of labourers, is unobstructed by shutters or bars; all is clean, quiet and attractive... When you pass the lodge, it is as if you had entered the precincts of some vast emporium of manufacture; labour is divided, so that it may be easy and well performed, and so apportioned, that it may suit the tastes and powers of each labourer. You meet the gardener, the common agriculturist, the mower, the weeder, all intent on their several occupations, and loud in their merriment. The flowers are tended, and trained, and watered by one, the humbler task of preparing the vegetables for table is committed to another.'

Victorian asylums sheltered and supported people with mental illness and learning difficulties. Each had its own community, based on a great building,

Opposite page: In these fancy dress costumes for a ball at Brookwood Asylum a great effort was made to be topical and comical, but it is unclear whether they were for patients or staff. (*Illustrated London News*, 1867.)

Sussex Asylum at Haywards Heath (built 1856–9) was a typical Victorian asylum. Male patients lived in one half and females in the other. A central administration block contained the Medical Superintendent's residence, and airing courts were laid out as gardens for the patients. The chapel and a tall water tower stood by the entrance gates.

park and gardens, and was intended to be therapeutic and to help cure the patients. Asylums spread throughout Britain, and their number grew rapidly during Queen Victoria's reign (1837–1901). In the fifty years between 1859 and 1909, the general population roughly doubled, but the number of 'persons of unsound mind' in institutions (including asylums and workhouses) quadrupled. In 1847 in England and Wales there were 5247 pauper patients housed in twenty-one publicly funded asylums. By 1914 this had risen to 108,837 patients in 102 asylums: an increase of eighty-one major buildings in sixty-seven years, with over one thousand patients per institution on average.

Asylums had spread through much of the world by 1914, but most have become redundant. Many survived into the late twentieth century as working

The second Surrey Asylum at Brookwood, near Woking (built 1862–7), in its heyday was reminiscent of a picturesque Italian hilltop town. The extensive buildings were grouped together on a vast scale. They created an easily recognisable asylum image described graphically in *The Builder* magazine in 1892: 'From any of the great main lines of railway which run through the shire, a traveller will be sure to spy, in some comparatively secluded position, a great group of buildings, which by their modern air and their tall chimney stacks, and possibly their bulky water-tower, seem to belong rather to the busy town than to country seclusion.'

Asylums were built in Scotland and Ireland, the British Empire and throughout the continent of Europe. In the United States of America asylums were often very large. The 120-bed Crichton Royal Hospital (depicted in 1847) was built outside Dumfries, Scotland, and opened in 1839 with W. A. F. Browne as its first medical director. It was the centre of moral therapy in Scotland and its busy regimen was based on 'kindness and occupation'.

psychiatric hospitals treating patients, many of whom lived in them for years, and for whom they were home. Better medication and other treatments brought obsolescence from the 1960s. After a century or more of service, nearly all Victorian asylums have now closed and their sites and buildings have been sold; most have been lost or changed beyond recognition. Few people outside the local communities near the asylums noticed or cared about the loss of such a rich strand of Britain's social, medical, architectural and landscape heritage.

Please note that in this book historic terms such as 'lunatic', 'insane', 'idiot' and 'asylum' are used as they were in the Victorian period, before they had acquired their current pejorative connotations. Definitions are approximate but in general 'lunatic' and 'insane' refer to those with mental illness; 'imbecile' and 'idiot' were used to describe those with learning difficulties. An 'asylum' is here taken to mean an institution devoted to housing the above classes of patient.

Bethlem Royal Hospital, St George's Fields, Southwark, London, mid nineteenth century. This building replaced the pioneering seventeenth-century one at Moorfields in 1815. Again, it was a magnificent edifice but it had more extensive and well-kept grounds for patients. The building became the Imperial War Museum in 1936. The long wings were removed, but the great cupola remains. (© Bethlem Art and History Collections Trust.)

EARLY ASYLUMS: FROM BEDLAM TO MORAL THERAPY

THE first purpose-built building devoted to insane patients was the Bethlem Hospital (erected 1674–6), usually known as Bedlam Hospital. Until the nineteenth century most of the insane were treated at home or found their way into prisons and hospitals. Bethlem Hospital was a pioneering charitable institution, founded in 1247, whose governors were determined to advertise their philanthropic enterprise when they required a new building in the late seventeenth century.

Bethlem, when it re-opened on a new site in 1676, was the most impressive building in the City of London. It stood just outside the London Wall and was, as John Evelyn remarked, 'most sweetly placed in Moorfields' for its country air and views. Designed by the fashionable architect Robert Hooke, it was nearly 500 feet (150 metres) long and overlooked the Moorfields promenade and park and the countryside beyond (now Finsbury Circus). The external architecture, scale and ornamentation were reminiscent of country houses such as Chatsworth, and even royal palaces, such as Sir Christopher Wren's work at Hampton Court.

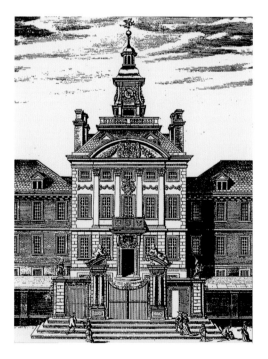

The showy, palatial exterior belied the spartan interior. The two main floors each had a long gallery as a day room, off which opened individual cells, 12 feet by 8 feet (3.7 by 2.4 metres). The 120 or more patients slept in their cells at night on straw palliasses, but those who were too dangerous were confined to their cells even by day. 'Heroic treatments' based on

purges, vomits and blood-letting, and less invasive cold and warm bathing, were common but generally ineffective. The asylum was essentially a holding ground for difficult patients. Even so, it was important for patients to have access to fresh air, so the building had two walled yards, known as airing courts, where they took exercise.

Notoriety arose from sightseers viewing patients in their distress. In 1753 a visiting journalist wrote: 'to my great surprize I found a hundred people at least, who having paid their two-pence apiece, were suffered unattended to run rioting up and down the wards, making sport and diversion of the miserable inhabitants…' Bethlem became the best-known and most notorious asylum, and 'Bedlam' has remained a byword for chaos.

Treatment of the insane became less oppressive as philosophers began to place faith in the power of human reason to transform and improve the world. During the eighteenth century doctors started to recommend greater personal freedom for insane patients. William Battie, the leading mad-doctor did not find medication of much use in curing. He believed that the regimen was more important in insanity than in any other illness. Confinement in an institution became an accepted part of this treatment and the therapeutic role of employment and exercise grew.

Asylums were only slowly constructed during the eighteenth century, and all were charitably funded. Bethlem was followed by Bethel in Norwich in 1712–13, and a further nine followed. They were close to regional centres

Bethlem Hospital was the first purpose-built asylum. Its style and ornament were fashionable for important buildings. But this palace for the mad was poorly built and skimped on accommodation: its long wings were only one room deep. The patients were not allowed into the large forecourt but had their own airing courts to the left and right. The smart Moorfields promenade in front enhanced the image of the institution but patients were not allowed out to use it. (© Bethlem Art and History Collections Trust.)

William Hogarth set the eighth and final view of his moral series *The Rake's Progress* in Bedlam, where Tom Rakewell reaped his final reward for a degenerate life. Here he is manacled in the communal gallery among paying onlookers and other patients, before dying among the lunatics. An aristocratic lady and her maid stand by, amused and disgusted by the antics of the unfortunate people around them. (© Bethlem Art and History Collections Trust.)

such as York, Hereford, Newcastle and Manchester, on the outskirts of town on cheap land, although urban sprawl soon engulfed them. The buildings were smaller and less impressive than Bethlem, which was used as a model. A private-sector 'trade in lunacy' grew rapidly, with asylums in private houses taking insane patients sent there and paid for variously by their relations and by the parish authorities. The treatment of most patients in asylums was notoriously brutal, partly for economic reasons as well as therapeutic.

'Raving Madness' statue from the Bethlem gateway, sculpted by by Caius Gabriel Cibber, 1670s. This statue, and its pair, 'Melancholy Madness', represent typical views of madness at the time and are the only remains of Robert Hooke's building. They are now at the Bethlem Royal Museum. (© Bethlem Art and History Collections Trust.)

'Moral therapy' appeared towards the end of the eighteenth century, and reflected in some ways Battie's belief that 'management [of patients] did much more than medicine'. Patients were encouraged to self-restraint in their behaviour, which was intended to lead to self-discipline. This dictated the regime at The Retreat, a pioneering Quaker charitable asylum in York, built in the mid 1790s. The Tuke family, who ran it, used humanity, reason and kindness, combined with restraint only where absolutely necessary. Medical intervention was minimised, particularly physical coercion and purgatives. The building and grounds were small-scale, and referred to as 'the house'. The routine was intended to be as domestic as possible, to remind patients of their home life and show them how to behave acceptably in such surroundings. The new idea was to reintegrate them into the family, particularly in Quaker ways, by walking, talking, and social and domestic activities such as taking tea with the Superintendent and his family. At The Retreat patients were encouraged to work and take exercise; a small farm and garden provided fresh air, which was still believed to be important. Physical exertion while working and exercising in the grounds tired patients so that they were less disruptive, and it supposedly diverted their minds from irrational thoughts.

Other asylums were built from the 1790s based on this system. They were secluded in the countryside behind walls and hedges and set in parks to ensure the patients had peace and quiet. Sightseers were expressly forbidden. The most prestigious were private establishments for wealthy and important patients and included Brislington House, Bristol (1804–6), built by the

The Retreat, York (built in the mid 1790s), was a pioneer of humane treatment set up by a Quaker family, the Tukes. A domestic-style building and regime helped to cure the patients. The purpose-built asylum looks much like a merchant's villa. The ideas developed here formed the basis for the ideals of treatment in the Victorian asylum. (From *Description of The Retreat*, 1813.)

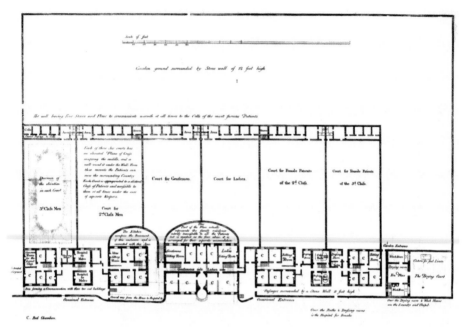

Brislington House, Bristol (built 1804–6), was a private asylum that specialised in the innovative and humane 'moral treatment'. The building had detached ward blocks, with a row of isolation cells at the back of the airing courts. The six patient blocks flanking the main block were divided by sex, with men to the left and women to the right. Patients were then housed by social class rather than by type of illness. This plan of c.1806 is perhaps the earliest surviving plan of a purpose-built asylum.

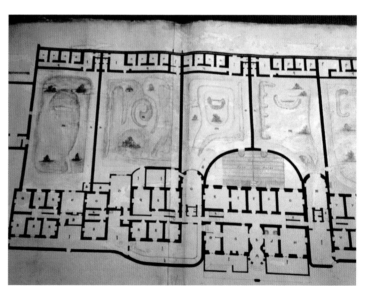

At Brislington House each walled airing court was laid out differently as a garden with a mount to take in views of the Bath hills. This was to help the patients recover their sanity. This beautiful and unique watercolour plan, prepared in 1843, shows the ornamental features of each court.

Ticehurst House, Sussex, was, like Brislington House, a private asylum for wealthy patients. The grounds had many elegant garden buildings in various styles, such as this pagoda, a moss house and a Gothic summerhouse, all illustrated in the publicity brochure of 1828.

Quaker Doctor Fox, and Ticehurst House, Sussex (1790s). The son of the murdered Prime Minister, Spencer Perceval, was a patient at both in the early nineteenth century and wrote an account of his treatment and the regime (which was not at all complimentary). This approach became the foundation for the Victorian asylum movement.

The Lincoln Asylum was built in 1820 as a 'public receptacle for objects suffering under the greatest of all human calamities'. The doctors of Lincoln County Hospital felt there was a need for a separate hospital for the mentally ill and a charitable subscription was raised to pay for it. It opened with only twelve patients but had 145 by 1852. It is now a conference centre called The Lawn.

GENERAL PLAN *of the* PAUPER LUNATIC ASYLUM
for
MIDDLESEX.

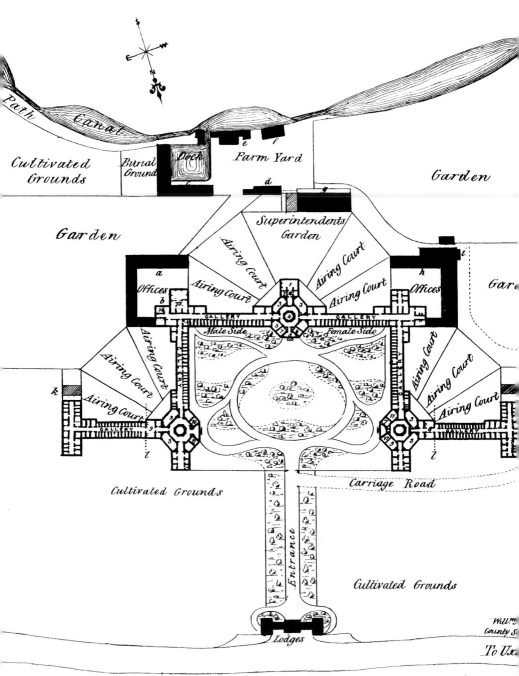

Path

Canal

Cultivated Grounds

Burial Ground

Dock

Farm Yard

e *f*

a

g

Garden

Garden

Superintendents Garden

Airing Court

Airing Court

Airing Court

Airing Court

a

Offices

b

GALLERY

Male Side

Female Side

GALLERY

h

Offices

i

Gar

Airing Court

Airing Court

Airing Court

Airing Court

k

Airing Court

GALLERY

GALLERY

l

l

Airing Court

Airing Court

Cultivated Grounds

Carriage Road

Entrance

Cultivated Grounds

Lodges

Will.m
County S

To Ux

BUILDING THE
ASYLUM TO CURE

THE royal 'madness' of George III (probably porphyria, a metabolic illness) raised public and parliamentary interest in the treatment of lunatics from the 1780s. The king's doctor, Dr Willis, did not, however, favour the mild methods employed at The Retreat.

Parliament passed the Lunatics Act in 1808, which permitted county magistrates to fund new asylums from the rates. The Act stipulated an airy position, at the edge of the urban centre, close to medical assistance; this differed little from earlier asylums. Patients began to be classified according to their symptoms as well as by gender. Twenty or so publicly funded asylums for paupers were built up to 1845 and largely followed the architecture and treatment set by The Retreat and developed at Brislington House. The difficulty was that the essential domestic approach was lost at a public asylum, which was built on a larger scale, for several hundred patients, with economy as a major factor.

The greatest early asylum superintendent was Dr (later Sir) William Ellis. He made his name at the first Yorkshire Asylum, in Wakefield (1816–18), which was influenced by Samuel Tuke from The Retreat. This impressive building was set in its own park, surrounded by a belt of trees and reached along a drive with a lodge. Numerous walled airing courts provided outdoor space for exercise without allowing the patients to escape (always a problem for asylums). Ellis moved, with his wife as matron, to the new Middlesex Asylum at Hanwell, opened in 1831. Both were prestigious public institutions at the forefront of their field and served fast-growing urban and industrial populations. In his *Treatise on the Nature, Symptoms, Causes and Treatment of Insanity* (1838) Ellis described and illustrated the Middlesex Asylum, including a plan of its layout, and set out an account of his regime.

Asylums were further endorsed when the 1845 Lunatics Act made counties provide for pauper lunatics. The numbers of the insane were growing as fast as or even faster than asylums could be built. Work and medical therapy were not effective and cures were few. However, asylum builders were not put off and there was a great boom in asylum building from the middle of the nineteenth century. Edward Charlesworth of Lincoln

The first Middlesex Asylum, Hanwell, was the largest asylum of all when it was built to serve London in 1828–31. William Ellis (1780–1839) and his wife set up the asylum as Superintendent and Matron after their establishment of the pioneering Yorkshire Asylum at Wakefield. The magnificent approach to the building set an example for the many later asylums. Ellis published this plan in his book on treating insanity to illustrate an ideal institution for the purpose. (From *Treatise on the Nature, Symptoms, Causes and Treatment of Insanity*, 1838.)

Edward Charlesworth (1783–1853) was an innovator in the early days of the Lincoln Asylum with his views on the benefits of treating patients without mechanical restraint. If it was absolutely necessary to place a patient in a restraint such as a strait jacket, he ensured that the person was accompanied by a nurse until the device was removed. This statue is at The Lawn, Lincoln.

Asylum was the first to publish on the benefits of treating patients without mechanical restraint. A young Scottish doctor, John Conolly, developed Ellis's pioneering work at Middlesex and took up Charlesworth's theories. Conolly wrote two seminal books which guided asylum builders: *The Construction and Government of Lunatic Asylums* (1847), and *The Treatment of the Insane without Mechanical Restraints* (1856). Although he was not the first to adopt this approach, he was the most effective publicist for the benefits of the asylum run without physical restraint using manacles, strait jackets and other devices.

The 1845 Lunatics Act saw the creation of a central lunacy inspectorate, in the Lunacy Commission, responsible for visiting and inspecting asylums. They laid down procedures for admitting patients to asylums, with the aim of avoiding malpractice and unnecessary committal. Fear of illegal detention was common and this act theoretically made committal more objective and better scrutinised. Patients admitted to private asylums had to have a statement of medical and social history, signed by the person asking for admission. Two detailed medical statements were also required confirming the person was 'an insane person or an idiot or a person of unsound mind'. The request for a pauper patient to be admitted to an asylum had to have similar justification and also be signed by a magistrate or clergyman of the parish, and by the Poor Law receiving officer or overseer. The legislation was amended later in the century to become even more stringent. A Parliamentary Select Committee in 1877 examined the lunacy law 'so far as regards security afforded for it against violations of personal liberty.' It found that serious abuses of inappropriate committal were not significant, but even so public concerns remained, and in 1890 the Lunacy Act made admission procedures still tighter to prevent collusion between those certifying patients.

Generally, discharge was regulated by the Committee of Visitors of the asylum, composed chiefly of magistrates who superintended the running of the asylum, and who were advised by the Medical Superintendent. Casebooks were kept detailing each patient's condition on admission, a record of discharge, and sometimes treatment although with the pressure of fast increasing numbers the treatment record was not always kept up to date. Few patients were released as 'cured', admissions increased and so the county pauper asylums became so-called warehouses for the mad. However, by the nineteenth century Bethlem Hospital, still a charitable institution, took only short-stay patients and was unlikely to take anyone considered incurable.

To try and prevent abuses within asylums, those in England and Wales were inspected by Commissioners in Lunacy, who were even able to visit by night and inspect all buildings and outhouses as well as records. They could discharge patients, if they felt it was necessary, after two visits seven days apart. At Surrey Asylum, Wandsworth, it was believed that abuses could only be minimised by the attendants having a constant fear of inspection. Thus in the 1870s medical officers of the asylum visited the wards unexpectedly by day and night.

New asylum buildings grew larger and larger, with many wards, connected via long corridors to a central administrative and service core. The small-scale domestic atmosphere which was at the heart of The Retreat's pioneering regime was lost. One great icon was the second Middlesex Asylum at Colney Hatch, in north London. It was opened in an atmosphere of hope by Prince Albert, the Prince Consort, in 1851, the year of the Great Exhibition in Hyde Park. Although the asylum was vast and externally palatial, and benefited from royal patronage, it was poorly built, like Bethlem, and did not achieve as many cures as expected. Its great corridor was a quarter of a mile (400 metres) long, with a parallel service

Left: John Conolly (1794–1866), resident physician of the first Middlesex Asylum 1839–44, took the post as a young man shortly after Ellis had retired. He was determined to make his name at this, the most prestigious public asylum, where he implemented and developed Charlesworth's ideas on abolishing mechanical restraint. This engraving shows a mild and good-humoured face, although Conolly was also a determined and ambitious man.

17

The second Middlesex Asylum at Colney Hatch (built 1849–51) in north London was even larger than the first at Hanwell. Built for over one thousand London patients, its third of a mile long classical façade exceeded even the length of Bethlem. It was opened by Prince Albert in 1851 and had large ornate grounds by a prestigious designer, William Broderick Thomas. (*Illustrated London News*, 1849.)

corridor in the basement. The walled, park-like grounds were laid out by the prestigious designer William Broderick Thomas, who also worked at Sandringham, the country house in Norfolk of Edward, Prince of Wales, as well as at other country house estates. The building was guarded by a grand lodge and gateway, with a mortuary and cemetery adjacent, and a broad avenue leading to the imposing main entrance.

Official advice for public asylum builders was provided by the Commissioners in Lunacy, based on Conolly's books. Their slim pamphlet was cumbrously entitled *Suggestions and Instructions in Reference to Sites: Construction and Arrangement of Buildings: Plans: of Lunatic Asylums* (1856). They

Serving a small rural county, the Buckinghamshire County Asylum (built 1850–3) opened at Stone near Aylesbury shortly after the metropolitan Colney Hatch. It was much smaller, built for two hundred patients and, as this postcard shows, had fewer pretensions to grandeur. However, it provided similar facilities and an attractive, almost homely entrance for newly arriving patients and visitors.

made recommendations which were already commonly used, and they stipulated a generous area of grounds to be provided per patient (four patients per acre). As this pamphlet was addressed at construction the Commissioners did not detail the medical treatment, although they took a keen interest in this key aspect when they visited asylums and reported in detail on regimes. They did, however, demand that land should be provided for therapeutic activities, including agricultural employment, exercise and recreation. Views were important for patients' therapy, both from the building and the grounds, together with a rural setting, and attractive grounds and airing courts.

Many lunatics lived in workhouses, but by the 1840s it was widely believed that the best place for them was in a purpose-built asylum. There was a rush to build asylums, and as soon as a county had constructed one it quickly became full, whereupon they erected a second and then a third asylum. There were even more in the metropolis – London had eleven by 1914. Around 120 asylums were built throughout England and Wales. They had much in common with the great Victorian show houses of the aristocracy, which were surrounded by complex gardens and informal parks.

Surrey boasted fourteen major asylums by 1914 – more than any other county – although most of them housed patients from metropolitan London in the countryside. Among these was Britain's biggest group of asylums, the 'Epsom Cluster', where five asylums were built on a 1000 acre (450 hectare) site in the 1900s, including an epileptic colony. Industrial Yorkshire was close behind Surrey in its provision for lunatics, with thirteen large asylums.

These enormous building projects cost hundreds of thousands of pounds each and took up to five years to complete. Notable architects were

The State Criminal Lunatic Asylum, Broadmoor, Berkshire, opened in 1863 and was designed by Joshua Jebb, the architect of Pentonville Prison. It replaced the facility previously provided by Bethlem Hospital at St George's Fields, Southwark. The great buildings stood isolated in farmland at the top of a steep hill. Spectacular views over Berkshire and Surrey were intended to benefit patients. The hillside was laid out in great terraces leading down to a 12 acre (4.8 hectare) kitchen garden. (*Illustrated London News*, 1867.)

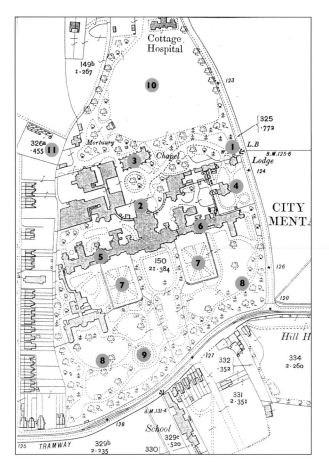

A typical asylum had a variety of buildings. The City of London Asylum, Stone, Kent (built 1862–6), included a chapel, mortuary and isolation hospital, shown on this Ordnance Survey map (1909). The grounds were elaborate, with a viewing mount, swirling paths, and 'Union Jack' plan paths through lawns. The estate included a cricket pitch and cemetery as well as farmland. Staff houses stood adjacent and the Superintendent had his own house and garden detached from the main building, next to the lodge.

KEY
1. Lodge and main gates
2. Main entrance and administration block
3. Chapel
4. Medical Superintendent's house and garden
5. Male wards
6. Female wards
7. Airing courts
8. Grounds for patients to use
9. Viewing mount
10. Cricket pitch
11. Kitchen garden

employed such as George Gilbert Scott (Wells, Somerset, 1845–8), who also designed country houses and workhouses; Joshua Jebb (the State Criminal Lunatic Asylum, Broadmoor, Berkshire, 1860–3), who also designed Pentonville Prison; and Arthur Blomfield (Chichester, 1894–7). Few architects designed more than one or two asylums, but G. T. Hine and C. H. Howell were official architects to the Commissioners in Lunacy and each designed several.

The architects used popular historic styles. Classical Greek Revival was favoured for early public asylums such as Lancaster (1818), Lincoln (R. Ingleman, 1819–20) and Hanwell (W. Alderson, 1828–31). Tudorbethan was popular in the 1840s and 1850s, and engagingly attractive, whether built of stone or brick, for example at Wells (G. G. Scott and W. B. Moffatt, 1845–8), Birmingham City Asylum (D. R. Hill, 1847–51) and the City of London

Asylum at Stone, Kent (J. B. Bunning, 1862–6). Gothic continued to be popular, for example Lancaster Annexe (T. Standen and A. Kershaw, 1882) and the Royal Albert Institution for Idiots (1866–73), also in Lancaster. By 1900 many asylums were designed in a simplified Queen Anne style, favoured by designers such as Richard Norman Shaw. These included Rauceby, Lincolnshire (G. T. Hine, 1897–1902), Napsbury, Hertfordshire (R. Plumbe, 1900–5), and Stannington, Northumberland (1910–14, G. T. Hine).

Above: Leavesden, Hertfordshire (built 1868–70), was unusual for its detached ward blocks and grid pattern of buildings and airing courts. However, it had all the same features as other asylums and was set in extensive grounds with a farm and cemetery. (From *The Builder*, July 1868.)

KEY
1. Main gates
2. Main entrance and administration block
3. Chapel
4. Kitchen, laundry, workshops
5. Water tower
6. Patients' ward – male blocks one side, female blocks the other
7. Corridor linking wards
8. Airing courts
9. Farmland and grounds for patients' recreation

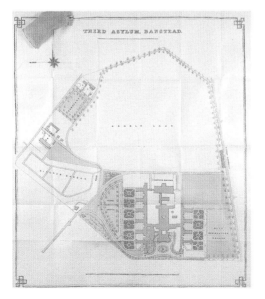

THIRD ASYLUM, BANSTEAD.

Right: The grounds were always laid out with great care so that the patients had a pleasant environment that might help them to recover. Alexander McKenzie drew up this attractive plan for Banstead Asylum, Surrey (built 1872–7). The building had the same layout as Leavesden. It was very unusual for two asylums to be based on the same design.

The testimonial to Robert Lloyd from Chichester Asylum Committee for his work in laying out the West Sussex asylum grounds, 1898. The Committee were so impressed that they awarded him this illuminated tribute.

The grounds were carefully landscaped, in some cases by important designers such as William Broderick Thomas (Colney Hatch) and Robert Marnock (Berkshire). William Goldring (Rauceby, Lincolnshire, and Napsbury, Hertfordshire) had an international landscape design practice. One man stands out as the most prolific asylum landscape designer: Robert Lloyd was Head Gardener at Brookwood Asylum, Surrey. He designed and supervised landscaping works at six asylums throughout England in the 1880s and 1890s, including Middlesbrough (1893–8), Chichester (1894–7) and St Albans (1896–9). At one guinea (£1.05) per day, plus payment for plans, Lloyd's fee was considerably lower than his main rival, Goldring, who charged 5 guineas, and this was presumably why Lloyd was employed more than any other designer. Goldring was, however, a more prestigious name for those asylum committees with less of an eye on the budget. Even so, Lloyd was competent and well regarded, and he was awarded an illuminated testimonial by the Chichester Asylum Committee in 1897 to record how highly they thought of his work.

The asylum building and estate were a key element of the therapeutic armoury. The asylum was a medical facility and was not intended to have a punitive regime with repressive and deterrent surroundings of the sort found in prisons and workhouses. To provide suitably cheering surroundings that would help lift the patients' mood, the asylum estate was modelled on the country house estate, with which it had much in common.

Essential elements of the asylum included lodges, drives, farms, trees, avenues, lawns, flower borders, shrubberies, ha-has, views, garden buildings, orchards and kitchen gardens. Ornamented airing courts were specific to asylums, opening off the wards so that patients had direct access to fresh air and exercise. Courts were usually provided with shelters, sometimes drinking fountains and even urinals for male courts, but patients were carefully supervised to ensure that no aggressive or antisocial behaviour occurred. Sport became important, and cricket and football pitches were

Above: Most asylums had lodges at the entrances to the estate. This one at the Somerset Asylum, Wells (1845–8), is in the same elaborate Tudor style as the main building. It helped the security of the estate to have a lodge and lodge keeper, deterring casual visitors and monitoring the movement of patients.

Below: The wooden gateway at Napsbury, Hertfordshire, opened in 1905, was guarded by a lodge. It was designed with considerable care in fashionable Arts and Crafts style.

MAIN : ENTRANCE : GATES :

Each asylum airing court usually had a shelter.

Above left: Napsbury had attractive thatched shelters, as did the earlier Brookwood, and a thatched cricket pavilion, which complemented the Arts and Crafts style gateway. It was cheaper to thatch the shelter roofs than use slate or tiles.

Above right: Rauceby, Lincolnshire (built 1897–1902), was a small rural asylum for an agricultural county. The airing court shelters reflected this modest character, although the landscape designer William Goldring provided an elaborate design for the grounds.

Right: Shelters were based on those used in public parks and seaside promenades. All had several seats facing different directions and were

screened so that patients could sit out of the wind at all times. At the private, fee-paying Cheadle Royal Asylum (built 1848–9) near Manchester especially grand shelters stood in the elaborate surroundings. Most other asylums were publicly funded.

Below: At the Somerset Asylum, Wells, the unusual shelters had central crenellated pavilions and encircling roofs which complemented the Tudor style of the building.

common, together with bowling greens. Water features were avoided where possible, and lakes were never constructed, partly because of their potential for suicides, but also because of their expense. Asylum cemeteries were provided in the grounds, especially where the parish churchyard was running out of space. Some cemeteries received several thousand patients; patients were not usually given individual headstones unless relations were prepared to pay and, as the inmates were mostly paupers, this seldom occurred. Cemeteries were grassy open spaces surrounded by walls and a gateway.

A railway connection was beneficial, for carrying supplies and visitors, after initial use during construction of the asylum. Some asylums had a station and a branch line off the main line into the building, such as at the Three Counties Asylum at Arlesey in Bedfordshire (1855–60), Hellingly in Sussex (1901–3) and Napsbury in Hertfordshire. The five asylums of the Epsom Cluster in Surrey were served by their own light railway and rolling stock, first for transporting building materials and then for bringing patients, visitors and supplies. The track was eventually taken up and sent for reuse in Nigeria, but the course of the line is still visible, with a country walk along part of it. The Cluster was also served by its own central power station and cemetery.

Inside, not surprisingly, the Victorian asylum, like Bethlem before it, was little like the large country house except for its warren of corridors and plethora of rooms. Male and female halves were divided into wards, each holding fifty to one hundred patients. Wards were allocated typically at Derby Asylum to classes such as 'Aged and Infirm', 'Moderately Tranquil' and 'Refractory'. Each ward had a day room with a dining area and individual single rooms. Some had dormitories where groups of quieter patients could be separated from the rest. All the main wards and day rooms were recommended to face south, so that patients benefited from maximum sunlight even indoors, and overlooked their airing courts. Photographs show that homely touches were introduced, such as carpet runners, table cloths and embroidered antimacassars, with pot plants on tables, and pictures on the walls. Homeliness was to be striven for, rather than the oppressiveness so likely in large institutions.

Central buildings included a recreation hall, chapel, dining hall, and facilities for therapeutic work: farm and workshops for male patients, and laundry and kitchen for females. Water was used in large quantities for domestic activities and for patients' use, and a large reservoir was required in case of fire. A tall ornamental water tower fulfilled these needs and dominated what came to resemble a rambling town. Early in the nineteenth century, the asylum

Drinking fountains were sometimes provided in airing courts. This one at Cheadle Royal is made of cast iron. Urinals could also be provided in male airing courts, for example at Middlesbrough.

superintendent lived at the centre of the main building, for example at The Retreat, York, and the first Middlesex Asylum, Hanwell. By the end of the century, the more modern superintendent was given his own substantial house and gardens in the grounds, maintained by patients, for example at Brookwood, Napsbury and Rauceby.

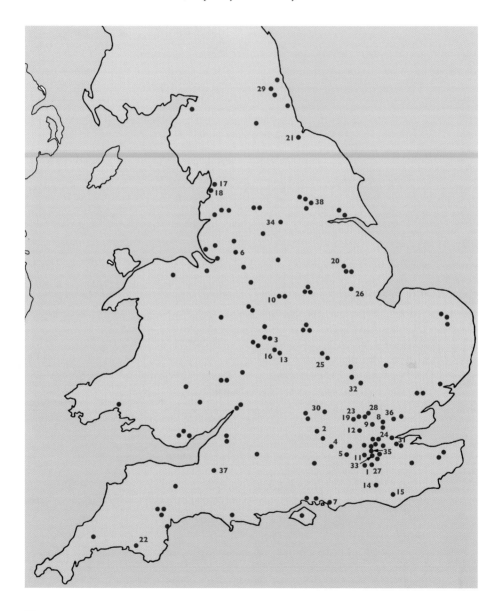

The form of the main building altered later in the century. The characteristic straight corridor, with wards and other large rooms leading off at right angles, was replaced by two corridors swept back at an angle from the central core in echelon form. Other elements were scattered in the grounds, including the isolation ward for infectious diseases, chapel and medical superintendent's house.

A bowling green was part of the superior facilities provided at Cheadle Royal Asylum for the private patients.

Left: Map showing the major asylums in England and Wales in 1914 (numbered locations are mentioned in this book). Asylums were scattered throughout England and in the north and south of Wales. There was a large concentration in Surrey, catering for London; others clustered around urban and industrial areas further north, particularly the West Riding of Yorkshire.

KEY TO MAP
1 Banstead (third Middlesex Asylum)
2 Berkshire Asylum (Fairmile)
3 Birmingham (City of Birmingham Asylum, All Saints)
4 Broadmoor (State Criminal Lunatic Asylum)
5 Brookwood (second Surrey Asylum)
6 Cheadle Royal Asylum (Manchester Royal Lunatic Hospital; private)
7 Chichester (West Sussex Asylum)

8 Claybury (fourth Middlesex Asylum)
9 Colney Hatch (second Middlesex Asylum)
10 Derby (Derbyshire Asylum)
11 Epsom Cluster (sixth, seventh, tenth, eleventh LCC Asylums and LCC Epileptic Colony, Ewell)
12 Hanwell (first Middlesex Asylum)
13 Hatton (Warwickshire Asylum)
14 Haywards Heath (Sussex Asylum)
15 Hellingly (East Sussex Asylum)
16 Knowle (Midland Counties Idiot Asylum)
17 Lancaster (Lancashire Asylum)
18 Lancaster (Royal Albert Institution for Idiots; charitable)
19 Leavesden (Metropolitan Asylum for Imbeciles)
20 Lincoln Asylum (The Lawn; charitable)
21 Middlesbrough (Borough Asylum)

22 Moorhaven (Plymouth Borough Asylum)
23 Napsbury (Middlesex Asylum)
24 New Bethlem, Southwark (charitable)
25 Northampton General Asylum (charitable)
26 Rauceby (Kesteven Asylum)
27 Royal Earlswood Idiot Asylum (charitable)
28 St Albans (Hertfordshire Asylum, Hill End)
29 Stannington (Gateshead Borough Asylum)
30 Stone (Buckinghamshire County Asylum)
31 Stone, Kent (City of London Asylum)
32 Three Counties Asylum, Arlesey (Fairfield)
33 Tooting Bec
34 Wakefield (first Yorkshire Asylum)
35 Wandsworth (first Surrey Asylum)
36 Warley (Essex Asylum)
37 Wells (Somerset Asylum)
38 York (The Retreat)

LIFE IN THE ASYLUM

PATIENTS

Patients were admitted for a variety of reasons, set out in the asylum's annual report. These included causes which are relevant today, such as stress, physical trauma and child-bearing (post-natal depression); others were less definable mental health problems, such as 'eccentricity'. Some we would not now regard as mental illness, such as epilepsy and imbecility (learning difficulties).

Living conditions were more comfortable than in the average working home and provided considerably more than the bare necessities that many were used to. Modern facilities abounded and included water closets, running water, gas or electric light, clothes, and warm, clean, spacious and ornamented surroundings. A constant supply of wholesome and varied food was provided, with beer, cocoa and tea to drink. Conolly admitted that an unvarying diet was not liked by patients, 'change of diet seeming to be desired, and even required, by patients of every [medical] class'. At Hanwell in 1848 he prescribed for male patients 247.5 ounces (around 15.5 pounds or 7 kg) of solid food per week and 15 pints (8.5 litres) of fluids, divided between breakfast, lunch, tea and supper. Extra rations of meat were provided for those working, or who were elderly, feeble or in infirmaries.

This comparative luxury was tempered by the regime and the close proximity to other patients. Each patient lived with up to fifty others with mental health problems in a ward under an authoritarian system. Privacy was minimal: eating and sleeping were communal, with a large dining hall and dormitories for thirty to fifty patients; beds were placed close together, and there was little personal space. The day was strictly regulated and managed by staff who were of varying competence and temperament. Patients had little say in their activities and none in their companions. Friends and relations were not usually prevented from visiting but could do so only at regulated times. Most asylums had strict visiting hours, with some of little more than two to four hours per day or restricted to certain weekdays. Visits

Opposite:
Brookwood male attendants in front of the airing court shelter.

29

Patients were sometimes photographed at their admission and again on their discharge. The two photographs above, from a series taken at Bethlem in the 1850s, show the same patient, Emma Riches, the first while suffering from 'puerperal mania', the second in convalescence. The second pair of photographs are of a male patient and were taken at Bethlem in the 1850s, the first when William Green was suffering from 'acute mania', the second when convalescent. (© Bethlem Art and History Collections Trust.)

might be stopped in specific cases when patients' friends and families were barred temp-or-arily, such as if a patient was in seclusion or suicidal, or if visitors had misbehaved, for example supplying banned items or substances such as alcohol. Visitors found that the remote location of the asylum in the countryside made it difficult and expensive to travel there. Patients became isolated from their own communities and institutionalised, depend-ent on the asylum for all their needs.

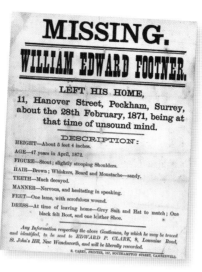

MISSING.
WILLIAM EDWARD FOOTNER.

LEFT HIS HOME,
11, Hanover Street, Peckham, Surrey, about the 28th February, 1871, being at that time of unsound mind.

DESCRIPTION:

HEIGHT—About 5 feet 4 inches.
AGE—47 years in April, 1872.
FIGURE—Stout; slightly stooping Shoulders.
HAIR—Brown; Whiskers, Beard and Moustache—sandy.
TEETH—Much decayed.
MANNER—Nervous, and hesitating in speaking.
FEET—One lame, with scrofulous wound.
DRESS—At time of leaving home—Grey Suit and Hat to match; One black felt Boot, and one leather Shoe.

Any Information respecting the above Gentleman, by which he may be traced and identified, to be sent to EDWARD P. CLARK, 8, Lorraine Road, St. John's Hill, New Wandsworth, and will be liberally rewarded.

E. CAREY, PRINTER, 187, SOUTHAMPTON STREET, CAMBERWELL.

The regime did not allow patients to leave the asylum without permission until they were judged ready for discharge. This poster was an attempt to retrieve an absconder from Brookwood Asylum.

Dormitories were often crowded, with beds close together, as in the female ward at Broadmoor. There was little room for personal possessions or space and the décor was sparse. It must have been difficult to sleep well close to so many other patients. (*Illustrated London News*, 1867.)

This selection of restraints shows the kind of items used to prevent patients from harming themselves or others when they could not be calmed. Their use was officially minimised and frowned upon by medical superintendents, and by writers such as John Conolly and Edward Charlesworth.

TREATMENT

Asylums adopted a plethora of new medical treatments but these were no more successful than the heroic blood-letting depletions, emetics and purgatives that were gradually abandoned. New treatments included chemicals with strong effects, including injections of morphia, as well as bromides, chloral hydrate, hyoscine, cannabis, amyl nitrate, digitalis and ergot. In melancholia, control of the digestive system was often regarded as the key to a cure. Mild purgatives such as rhubarb were favoured. Opium was used to calm excited patients. Non-chemical methods included the application of electricity, the Turkish bath, and hot and cold shower baths. Doctors could not agree on treatment, largely because of the ineffectiveness of these methods. One of the key Victorian medical texts (*A Manual of Psychological Medicine*, 1858) admitted that active medicinal treatment was useless, especially in 'chronic' cases. Its authors, Tuke and Bucknill, noted that 'any active medicinal interference is more likely to do harm than

Harness combinations from Brookwood Asylum, now at the Woking Lightbox museum. This mid to late nineteenth-century item of clothing would be used in conjunction with a strong dress or padded suit if a particularly aggressive patient needed restraint.

good'. The dismal lack of medical success led to moral therapy being used as the treatment with the most potential for cures.

The use of mechanical restraints sometimes could not be avoided in order to prevent injury while a patient was agitated and violent. Padded restraining garments were used. Padded cells were provided within wards where violent patients could be isolated without harming themselves until their mania subsided.

The longer a patient stayed in an asylum the less likelihood there was of his or her release, and a growing proportion of the asylum population comprised chronic, long-stay patients. However, patients were not always confined for life. At asylums such as Brookwood and Lancaster it seems that one third or so were released in under a year.

PATIENTS' WORK

Patients' work was important and highly valued in the Victorian asylum, both for their well-being and recovery, and to maintain control. Many patients were unwilling to work and some were unable to because of their condition. Privileges were used to coax them, and their withdrawal might include depriving a man of his tobacco or enforced absence from balls, concerts and entertainments. Violent attendants were not unknown, but ill-treatment was strictly forbidden and not officially tolerated. Offenders were punished when identified.

Farming was a major part of the asylum estate economy and provided food for staff and patients, as well as therapeutic activity for male patients. This plan of the farm at Middlesbrough Asylum (built 1893–8) shows the estate crops distributed around the asylum.

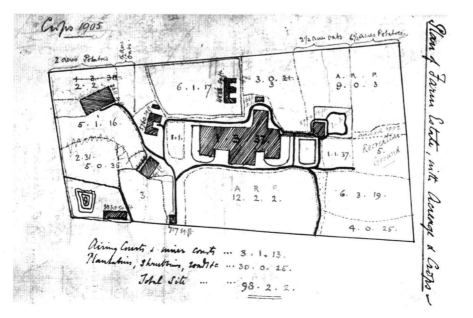

Most activities were gender-specific but some of the most mundane were given to men or women (although not in the same place). Picking lumps out of horsehair for mattresses was one; others were making coconut fibre mats, and rolling up slips of paper to stuff disposable pillows. Activities that moved the whole body were preferable, and outdoor occupations were favoured over indoor ones as more beneficial. Work on the land was the most highly valued by the medical staff, particularly farm work, but also garden work such as digging, hoeing, forking and carting for men, and for women, weeding, light hoeing and sorting potatoes.

Patients who worked in the fields (usually men) might be some distance from the farm or main buildings. When there was no drinking water nearby, they were provided with water flasks such as this early-twentieth-century example from Brookwood Asylum, now at The Lightbox museum, Woking.

The farm at the State Criminal Lunatic Asylum, Broadmoor, Berkshire, opened in 1863, supplied food for the four hundred patients for which it was designed (three hundred men, one hundred women). The type and quantity

Garden and farm produce, Broadmoor, 1865

quantity	item produced	value £	s	d
Garden				
97 bushels	French beans	19	8	0
24 bushels	peas	2	2	0
51 bushels	turnips	2	11	0
644 dozen	cabbages	32	4	0
302 dozen	lettuces	8	16	2
634 sticks	celery	2	12	10
842 pounds	marrows	1	15	0
15,804 pounds	rhubarb	32	18	6
150 bushels	greens	5	12	6
20 hundredweight	parsnips	4	0	0
28 1/2 hundredweight	carrots	4	19	9
297 sacks	potatoes	103	19	0
Farm				
1069	eggs	4	9	1
148 pounds	lard	5	11	0
2670 pounds	pork	89	0	4
120 pounds	mutton	4	0	0
4303 gallons	milk	179	6	0
Total value		503	5	2

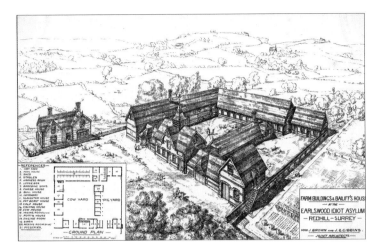

The farm at the Royal Earlswood Asylum in Surrey (built 1852–5) was used to train older boys to become farm labourers when they left the institution.

of produce was not unusual, except perhaps the quantity of rhubarb, which as a purgative was considered a useful therapeutic tool.

Small garden allotments for individuals were encouraged at the first Middlesex Asylum, Hanwell. They were believed to improve the patients' quality of life and to help them to recover. Hanwell's Matron reported on small gardens for the female patients in 1857:

'A most valuable, perhaps as yet an inappreciable remedial agent, has been… the establishment of a number of small Pleasure Gardens… separated and surrounded by gravel walks, and bordered with box; they are allotted to

The head gardener of each asylum managed a team of gardeners, mostly male patients. Robert Lloyd, head gardener at Brookwood, started his career at private gardens in Warwickshire. He is important as he designed the grounds of six other asylums. Here he is towards the end of his life in the 1890s.

individual Patients; and each is given up to the sole care and cultivation of its possessor, and bears her name, which is painted on an oval zinc plate, and placed in a conspicuous position. Some of the amateur gardeners display considerable artistic skill, as well as great taste in the arrangement of their plants and flowers; and the whole space thus occupied presented…, during the whole summer and autumn, a most interesting scene…. But not only has the physical health of many Patients become benefited by exercise in this new field of labour, its moral effects are undeniable. Reciprocal kindnesses are interchanged, mutual sympathies are elicited, and forbearance is in continual exercise.'

Little bouquets found their way from these gardens into the wards.

Some patients, particularly those from cities, did not want to work outdoors. They found gardening or agricultural work degrading, preferring to work indoors at cleaner and less arduous jobs. Men could work at artisan jobs in workshops for tailors, shoemakers, upholsterers, carpenters and blacksmiths. Women worked in the laundry and kitchen or at needlework for patients' clothes.

Indoor tasks for patients were used in the early stages of recovery, progressing to outdoor tasks if possible. John Rutherford, a Northumberland coal miner, was admitted to the county asylum in June 1890. When he showed 'small signs of improvement' from the 'idle and acute stage' he was put to work in the flock-picking room, the first step to full employment (and not a pleasant activity). By October he worked in the grounds, being

The asylum laundry at Brookwood was a well-organised operation. This photograph of 1906 shows that it was staffed by crisply attired female patients and staff, using modern, industrial-scale equipment.

The female day rooms at Brookwood were typical in their homely touches, with gay colour schemes, pictures on the walls, pot plants, and crocheted tablecloths and chair covers.

Croquet in the men's airing court, Broadmoor. This game was approved for men and women, although the use of heavy mallets by criminal lunatics may have caused some disquiet. Broadmoor was built as an asylum not a prison and so did not have the same spartan and repressive regime as a prison, in which such activities would never have been allowed. (*Illustrated London News*, 1867.)

'industrious and much improved in every respect', and by November he was working outside daily and said to be mentally improved. In December he was discharged as recovered, but the cure was not permanent for he was re-admitted three times over the next few years.

Dangers were present at work: where supervision in workshops was not strict, sharp or heavy tools could used as weapons or for self-harm. Patients could be overworked if not fit enough to undertake tasks. Unsupervised 'mingling of the sexes' might lead to unwanted pregnancies, particularly where both sexes were employed in the same place, such as the kitchen or laundry.

AMUSEMENTS

Recreation was an essential part of treatment and a variety of amusements was provided. This was markedly different to the regimes of other institutions, such as prisons and workhouses, which were usually punitive.

Monogrammed china, including plates and mugs, was sometimes provided. This forms part of a collection, now at The Lightbox, made for Brookwood Asylum.

Activities were divided into those in the confines of the ward and airing court, and entertainments in the wider asylum for patients as performers or spectators. Patients' dances occurred through the year and were an exception to the general insistence on strict separation of the sexes. At the Three Counties Asylum, Bedfordshire, it was reported in 1861 that: 'entertainments were held every fortnight, in the evening, dancing, etc... also the band, formed by the attendants, forms a praiseworthy part of their duty for the patients' comfort: and at the Christmas parties an addition was made to the supper of sandwiches, cake etc... a representation of the "Ethiopian Serenaders" was got up by the attendants.' Flower shows and fêtes in the grounds were much enjoyed in summer.

On the ward, reading was encouraged and a liberal supply of newspapers

The day room for male patients at Broadmoor apparently provided various amusements, including draughts and tables for reading. This rather rosy scene seems more like a working men's club than a criminal lunatic ward. (*Illustrated London News,* 1867.)

The women's airing court at Broadmoor was planted as an ornamental garden, with a shelter, borders, lawns, paths and croquet. All the courts were surrounded by a very high wall. Today it seems an unusual subject for a postcard such as this.

was recommended. Female patients crocheted, knitted, and netted with twine for the gardens. Men could also do the last. Board games were provided. Activities in the airing courts included croquet, skittles, quoits, bowls, fives, lawn tennis and badminton, or just walking or sitting. Activities in the wider grounds included games, and walking parties were taken on prescribed routes through the park and into the countryside.

Sports were mainly for men; particularly popular were cricket and football. Sports facilities were laid out in the grounds, with patients doing much of the labouring. The cricket pitch usually had a pavilion and sometimes the outfield was grazed by the farm sheep. The wooden pavilion at Napsbury was thatched in a very attractive old English style to match the shelters in the airing courts.

Visitors were restricted to particular hours. At the Three Counties Asylum patients were allowed visitors on Mondays, Tuesdays, Wednesdays and Saturdays between 10 am and 4 pm and at

Brookwood Asylum

By the Trains leaving Waterloo Station by London and South Western Railway, for Brookwood,

At 6.15 a.m.,
At 10.15 a.m.,
At 2.25 p.m.,

Third Class Return Tickets
TO
Brookwood & Back
WILL BE ISSUED TO
Visitors to Patients in the County Asylum,
AT THE FARE OF
THREE SHILLINGS.

The Return Half of the Ticket MUST BE STAMPED AT THE ASYLUM BEFORE RETURNING, or the full Fare will be charged.

The Tickets are available for return on the day of issue, by Trains leaving Brookwood Station at 1.12, 6.44, & 8.59 p.m.
BY ORDER.

Visitors were usually admitted to the asylum on prescribed days and times. The method of travel was important, as most asylums were in the countryside and difficult to reach on foot. It was an advantage to have a nearby railway line with a station and at Brookwood discounted tickets were provided. Even so, three shillings (15p) was expensive when a typical weekly wage was one pound.

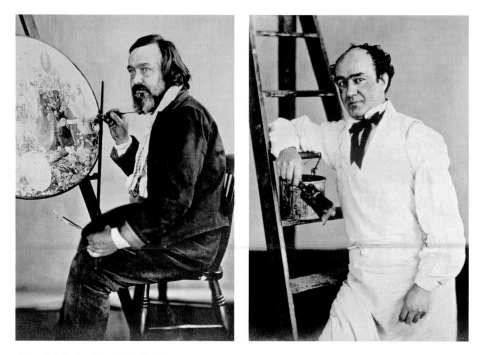

Above left: Richard Dadd (1817–86) was one of the most talented artists of his generation and continued painting while in Bethlem and then Broadmoor from 1844 to his death. Here he is in the 1850s painting one of his best works, 'Contradiction: Oberon and Titania', now in the Tate Gallery, based on his continued interest in the fairy world. (© Bethlem Art and History Collections Trust.)

Above right: Edward Oxford, at the age of eighteen, tried to shoot Queen Victoria in her carriage in Hyde Park in 1840. While in the Bethlem criminal department for the next twenty-four years, before his deportation to Australia, he studied many languages and became proficient in many skills. He became an expert house-painter and wood-grainer and is shown with his tools of the trade in this photograph. (© Bethlem Art and History Collections Trust.)

all times in cases of dangerous illness. Visitors of the opposite sex could not stay in a room with a patient unless a third person was present. Visitors often had difficulty reaching the rural asylums, although part of the purpose of the railway, if provided, was to transport visitors.

Artists and poets sometimes continued to produce notable work in the asylum. Some were well-known, others not, but their work has sometimes survived and can be very attractive. The artist Richard Dadd was in the criminal department of New Bethlem (in the building now occupied by the Imperial War Museum) from 1844 to 1864, and then for twenty-two years at Broadmoor, Berkshire. Jonathan Martin, the incendiary of York Minster, was a tanner by trade but proved to be a talented artist while in Bethlem from 1829 to 1838. The artist Louis Wain (1860-1939), famous for his quirky

Top left: Artistic talent expressed by patients could be treasured and preserved whoever the artist was. This beautiful watercolour study of a falcon remains bright and vibrant; it was painted at Brookwood in about the 1870s by a talented patient of no special fame or note. Many asylum archives retain works of art by their patients, proof of their creativity even in such an institution.

Top right: The feline drawings of the artist Louis Wain (1860–1939) were popular from the 1880s and he created a whole imaginary world of cat activities. He suffered from a dementia-type illness and spent his last years from 1924 in asylums, including Bethlem and Napsbury. He continued to draw and paint in the asylums, including cats, brightly coloured landscapes and other subjects. (© Bethlem Art and History Collections Trust.)

Left: Jonathan Martin (1782–1838) nearly burnt down York Minster. This text, beginning 'Oh England pere pare [prepare] to meet thy God', was written shortly after he entered Bethlem in 1829 and illustrated with a beautiful but thorny rose. (© Bethlem Art and History Collections Trust.)

Only attendants of the same sex were allowed to look after patients. Sometimes several generations of one family followed each other working at the asylum as attendants. The asylum was a significant employer in the area because of its need for many staff with different skills.

cartoons and sketches of cats, spent the end of his life with dementia in asylums, including Tooting Bec and Bethlem in London and Napsbury, Hertfordshire. The poems of Arthur Legent Pearce, a medical man who tried to murder his wife while in the grip of delusions, were published in 1851 while he too was incarcerated in New Bethlem. John Clare, the peasant poet, published *Poems Descriptive of Rural Life and Scenery* in 1820 when he was aged twenty-seven, but he was confined in the Northampton General Asylum for the last twenty-two years of his life, dying in 1864.

STAFF: WORK

At the top of the asylum hierarchy were the Superintendent, always a medical man, and his Matron. Early on it was common for the Superintendent's wife to be the Matron. The Superintendent reported to his Visiting Committee. This included prominent local men, such as magistrates, gentry and aristocrats, who had supervised the funding and building of the asylum

and ensured that it was run appropriately. The Superintendent's annual report provided a wealth of statistics, ranging from the causes of illness to the number of patients working in various parts of the asylum, and the value of asylum farm and garden produce. A chaplain took services in the asylum chapel, which was frequently provided, and he also reported annually. Other senior staff included the assistant medical officer, bailiff, and engineer; less prestigious positions included the head gardener and his staff, the lodge porter, and artisans running workshops.

The wards were staffed by attendants, who were not medically trained in the early days. Male and female staff were segregated as strictly as the patients and often lived in the asylum. They were difficult to recruit and tended to be of insufficient calibre. The usual proportion of attendants to patients was one to thirty, which made it difficult to ensure that patients were adequately cared for.

When the Surrey Asylum opened at Wandsworth in 1841 the Superintendent's salary was £150 a year and the Matron, who was in charge of the female wards and the female staff, was paid £80. Attendants rose at 6 am, to 'wash and comb' the patients, and reported any illness. At 8 am they served breakfast and cleaned the sleeping rooms, removing any foul straw or linen. They served meals at particular times, attended patients at specified intervals, and were forbidden to strike or ill-treat patients 'on pain of *instant dismissal*'. As the century progressed, training for attendants was instituted and prizes were sometimes awarded as an incentive for carrying out their duties properly.

The working parts of the asylum were staffed by specialist attendants, who not only ran their own area such as workshop or farm, but supervised working patients. Farms included the

Fire was always a threat. Buildings were designed to withstand it for as long as possible, with tall water towers to provide a source for tackling blazes, for example at Sussex Asylum, Haywards Heath. An asylum fire brigade with its own fire tender and other equipment was a source of great pride. This fire bucket and stirrup pump of the 1880s, now at The Lightbox, Woking, was used at Brookwood Asylum, where a 118 feet (36 metres) high water tower was built in 1885, holding 30,000 gallons (136,383 litres) of water. It was kept solely as a reservoir in case of fire. The fire brigade consisted of an engineer along with attendants and patients.

The Medical Superintendent in charge of the asylum was treated with great deference. This skilful sketch of Dr Brushfield, Superintendent at Brookwood, was made by a patient. One wonders how he got the Superintendent to sit for him.

Staff sports teams and bands provided entertainment for patients and staff. Competition between asylums, prisons and other institutions was stiff. This photograph shows the canine mascot adopted by the Brookwood football team of 1899.

whole range of animals, including heavy horses, and grew the usual variety of crops, both agricultural and market garden. Broadmoor's 12 acre (4.8 hectare) kitchen garden produced 15,000 pounds (6804 kg) of rhubarb for the asylum in one year in the 1860s.

Asylums had their own calendar of dates important to the institution, in which staff and patients were usually involved. However, the Sussex Asylum Commemoration Ball in 1863 was only for staff, as this programme notes.

SUSSEX LUNATIC ASYLUM,
HAYWARD'S HEATH.

THE FOURTH COMMEMORATION DAY
OF THE OPENING OF THE ASYLUM, IN 1859,

WILL BE HELD

On SATURDAY, JULY 25th, 1863.

ORDER OF THE DAY:—

11. 0 A.M.—MORNING PRAYER, with SERMON.—Preacher, the Rev. W. FITZ HUGH, M.A., Rector of Street.

12.15 P.M.—CRICKET—AUNT SALLY—TRAP, BAT, AND BALL—FOOT BALL, &c., &c.
1.30 „ —PATIENTS' DINNER ON THE GROUNDS—LUNCHEON FOR THE VISITORS.
2.15 „ —JUMPING IN SACKS, and WHEEL-BARROW RACE.
3. 0 „ —GLEES by the SINGING CLASS.
3.30 „ —READINGS in the RECREATION HALL, (by Mrs. PROSSER, of Brighton.)
4.30 „ —DANCING on the LAWN.
5.30 „ —PATIENTS' TEA ON THE GROUNDS—TEA FOR THE VISITORS.
6.30 „ —BALL in the RECREATION HALL.

To CONCLUDE AT EIGHT P.M.

The Asylum String Band will play the Dance Music, and the Asylum Brass Band will play numerous Airs during the Day.

THE COMMEMORATION BALL FOR THE HOUSEHOLD
Will be held in the RECREATION HALL, on MONDAY, the 27th JULY,
COMMENCING AT 8.30 P.M.

HAYWARD'S HEATH, JULY 16, 1863.

⁎ A Train leaves Brighton at 10.0 a.m., arriving at Hayward's Heath in time for the Chapel Service.
Trains return to Brighton at 7.37, 8.0, 8.10, and 9.12 p.m.

STAFF RECREATION
Many staff lived in the building or latterly in houses in the grounds. The staff community was large and close-knit and shared some of the facilities with the patients. The staff often held their own entertainments. A particularly rowdy one at the Three Counties Asylum, Bedfordshire, was noted in 1861, when eighty-nine people were present. It lasted until 6 am the following day and thirty-six bottles of wine and spirits were consumed (without

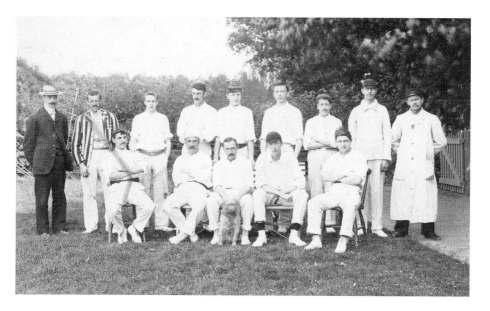

permission) from the medical stores, and 320 pints (182 litres) of beer. This amounted to 4 pints of beer and half a pint of spirits for every person present.

Football was one of the most popular sports played by both patients and staff at Gartloch Asylum, Glasgow, in the 1890s. Teams from the different

Asylum cricket team, Brookwood, late nineteenth century.

The asylum band, such as this one at Brookwood, provided music for various activities including dances and outdoor fêtes.

Social activities were provided to help patients recover, echoing early treatment at The Retreat, York. The band at this female dance at Broadmoor must have been formed by the male staff. The Superintendent and his female party look on in approval (far left). (*Illustrated London News*, 1867.)

areas of the hospital played each other and other hospitals. The 'married' team (made up of married male attendants) had memorable jousts with the 'single' team. Lawn tennis became popular. Sports days involved both staff and patients mingling on a less formal footing. Earlier, at the Three Counties Asylum in the 1860s only the staff played cricket, sang in the choir, played in the band or performed in the theatre, providing entertainment for the patients. Male patients watched cricket from their airing courts, which overlooked the cricket field.

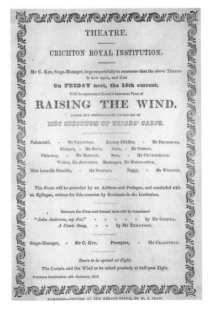

Concerts and theatricals were common in asylums, to provide light relief for patients and staff. At the Crichton Royal, Dumfries, Dr Browne placed great emphasis on entertainment for the patients. In 1843, for the first time ever in an asylum, his patients produced and performed a play, 'Raising the Wind'. This playbill shows that the hospital's benefactress, Mrs Crichton, was present at this momentous occasion.

SPECIALIST ASYLUMS

IDIOT ASYLUMS

The first major specialist asylum was the idiot children's asylum. By the 1850s it was recognised that it was inappropriate to keep children with learning disabilities alongside adult lunatics. An educational rather than a curative regime in a separate institution was more appropriate. The idiot children's asylum, although based on the pauper asylum model, was designed to be a long-term home as the children grew up. It was a less confined regime with a large central building laid out in gardens with playing fields and playgrounds. Two of the most impressive examples were the Royal Earlswood Idiot Asylum, Redhill, Surrey (1852–5), and the Royal Albert Institution for

Royal Earlswood Asylum for Idiots was one of the first institutions of its type and its foundation stone was laid by Prince Albert in 1853. (*Illustrated London News,* 1867.)

The Midlands Idiot Asylum was built at Knowle, Warwickshire. Laying the foundation stone of the asylum here in 1872 was a cause for great civic pride, typically marked by a ceremony for local and sometimes national dignitaries. (*Illustrated London News*, 1872.)

The Royal Albert Idiot Asylum, Lancaster (built 1866–73), was built to serve north-west England. With its massive water tower and great bulk it looked more like a great French château or town hall than a home for children. (*Illustrated London News*, 1876.)

Idiots, Lancaster (1866–73). The children were educated with the intention that they should acquire life skills that would help them when they became adults. Only seven or so were built, and most were charitably funded. Most other 'idiots' were housed in workhouses, especially those who did not disrupt the daily routine, or else remained in mainstream asylums.

EPILEPTIC COLONIES

The epileptic colony developed from the 1890s and showed the greatest divergence from the usual asylum structure. By this time fragmentation of buildings, to break them into smaller units within the institution, was

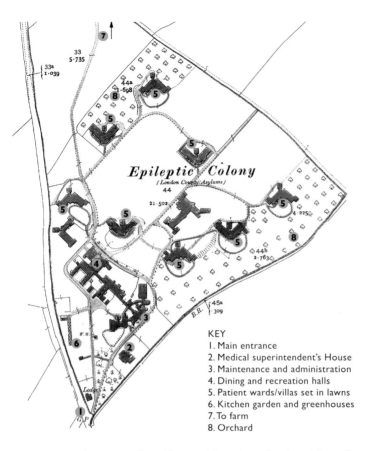

Epileptic Colony
(London County Asylums)
44
21·502

KEY
1. Main entrance
2. Medical superintendent's House
3. Maintenance and administration
4. Dining and recreation halls
5. Patient wards/villas set in lawns
6. Kitchen garden and greenhouses
7. To farm
8. Orchard

London County Council Epileptic Colony, Ewell, opened in 1903, was one of the Epsom Cluster of five asylums serving London. It housed epileptic patients, who, it was intended, should benefit from work on the estate or in the establishment. The patients lived in detached wards with their own gardens in a kind of garden city type layout, illustrated on this Ordnance Survey map. These were scattered among lawns and orchards and the men went to work on the farm some distance away. Few other examples were built, but this was the forerunner of the inter-war mental deficiency colonies set up by local authorities.

common in orphanages and workhouses. The colony developed from the medical belief that the most active epileptic patients would benefit from living in an institution adapted to their circumstances. Epileptic patients were isolated from those with mental illness, on separate sites in buildings of more domestic scale and character. The estate was intended to be tailored to the needs of epileptics by providing therapeutic work for the patients, either farm work or in workshops.

Instead of a great Hydra-like asylum building, the wards were separated by lawns in attractive grounds, linked by paths and drives and with their own gardens. This was reminiscent of the developing contemporary garden cities, such as Letchworth, Hertfordshire. The administration block and central services were housed in a large building rather like a town hall. The Arts and Crafts architectural style provided an attractive and homely setting. Ewell Epileptic Colony, Epsom, Surrey (1900–3), was a good example and was one of the Epsom Cluster.

THE LAST DAYS OF
THE ASYLUM

THE Victorian asylum has all but vanished. Asylum estates continued largely unchanged, even when taken over by the National Health Service (NHS) in 1948, until the 1990s, but the post-war world entertained more liberal ideas; new drugs brought more effective relief and enabled greater control of patients' condition without physical isolation in vast institutions. The 'open door' policy, in which greater freedom of movement was provided for patients, led to the unlocking of ward doors. Airing court walls and railings were removed. Farms where male patients worked were closed; prize stock herds and estate farmland were sold. Patients no longer cleaned wards or worked in kitchens and laundries. There was a perceived need in the mid twentieth century for 'therapeutic community systems' rather than large impersonal institutions: 'care in the community' was the new theory.

Most Victorian asylums became psychiatric hospitals but closed in the 1980s and 1990s. In 1995 the NHS predicted that over 120 major sites would become surplus and be sold, most of which were asylums. This left a huge problem of what to do with these large estates and unwieldy buildings to obtain the maximum return. They were ripe for redevelopment, but their historic and aesthetic value was often not recognised. The most cost-effective option was to demolish the buildings and build in the grounds as happened to some fine sites including the Buckinghamshire Asylum, Stone, and Brookwood Asylum, Woking. Some asylums have survived as working hospitals including Broadmoor, Berkshire and The Retreat, York (still a charitable institution).

A few exemplary schemes converted asylums to houses and apartments set in the attractive landscaped grounds, particularly where the building or grounds were important enough to be listed or registered. Their rambling nature means that buildings can be easily divided into many self-contained units without damaging the essential quality of the design. The grounds provide a high quality setting for the re-used buildings, valued by the new inhabitants. In conversion, however, the grounds often suffer more than the buildings as the ornamental airing courts and gardens are the most

Redundant asylums of special architectural importance have been reused, often for residential developments. Princess Park Manor has emerged from the second Middlesex Asylum at Colney Hatch, rescued by a sympathetic developer.

The fate of other asylums was not so rosy. Many such as Brookwood (here) and the Buckinghamshire Asylum were demolished to make way for large-scale housing or retail developments.

convenient place for parking. In rural areas the asylum farm and farmland usually survives, managed by local farmers. Asylum cemeteries are almost impossible to re-use and often become overgrown, lost and forgotten.

Good conversions include Colney Hatch, London, Claybury and Warley, Essex, Moorhaven, Devon, and Haywards Heath, West Sussex. At Colney Hatch the vast redundant and dilapidated asylum, by now engulfed in urban north London, was converted into prestigious apartments with 30 acres (12 hectares) of pleasure grounds including the main entrance, the original grand approach and the cemetery. Unfortunately the airing courts were lost but Broderick Thomas's pleasure ground has survived well and provides arcadian recreation for the new residents. Moorhaven, set idyllically at the edge of Dartmoor, has become a new tranquil village. The essential rural tranquility has been preserved along with the attractive sprawl of asylum buildings.

Asylum conversions occurred throughout Britain. Gateshead Asylum, Stannington (built 1910–14), set deep in the Northumberland countryside, was photographed in 2002 waiting to be developed for its new use.

FURTHER READING

The histories of many asylums have been written, often to celebrate their achievements, but may now be out of print. Local studies libraries are useful places to search for such books. The Wellcome Library in London provides an excellent source of out-of-print and current books on asylums and mental health, with an images database, manuscripts and archives.

The following selection highlights various aspects of the Victorian asylum:

Allderidge, P. *The Bethlem Royal Hospital: An Illustrated History.* Bethlem and Maudsley NHS Trust, 1995.

Andrews, J., et al. *The History of Bethlem.* Routledge, 1997.

Burdett, Charles Henry. *Hospitals and Asylums of the World*, volumes 1 and 2. London, 1893.

Gardner, J. *Sweet Bells Jangled Out of Tune: A History of the Sussex Lunatic Asylum (St Francis Hospital, Haywards Heath).* James Gardner, Brighton, 1999.

Hunter, R., and Macalpine, I. *Three Hundred Years of Psychiatry 1535–1860.* Oxford University Press, 1963.

Hunter, R., and Macalpine, I. *Psychiatry for the Poor. 1851 Colney Hatch Asylum.* Dawsons, 1974.

Hutton, G. *Gartloch Hospital 100 Years.* Richard Stenlake, 1994.

Jones, K. *Asylums and After: A Revised History of the Mental Health Services.* Athlone, 1993.

Michael, P. *Care and Treatment of the Mentally Ill in North Wales 1800–2000.* University of Wales Press, 2003.

Parry-Jones, W. L. *The Trade in Lunacy: A Study of Private Madhouses in England in the Eighteenth and Nineteenth Centuries.* Routledge, 1972.

Pettigrew, J., et al. *A Place in the Country: Three Counties Asylum 1860–1998.* South Bedfordshire Community Health Care Trust, 1998.

Porter, R. *Mind-Forg'd Manacles.* Penguin, 1990.

Porter, R. *Madness: A Brief History.* Oxford University Press, 2002.

Richardson, H. (editor). *English Hospitals 1660–1948: A Survey of Their Architecture and Design.* Royal Commission on the Historical Monuments of England, 1998.

Scull, A. *The Most Solitary of Afflictions: Madness and Society in Britain, 1700–1900.* Yale University Press, 1993.

Stevenson, C. *Medicine and Magnificence: British Hospital and Asylum Architecture, 1660–1815.* Yale University Press, 2000.

Tuke, S. *Description of The Retreat.* Process Press, 1996.

Williams, M. *History of Crichton Royal Hospital 1839–1989.* Dumfries and Galloway Health Board, 1989.

Contemporary journals include:

The Builder, 1846–1914 (many articles and illustrations relating to then-new asylums)

Journal of Mental Science, 1853–1914 (articles on treatment and asylums)

WEBSITES

The Hospital Records Database, a joint project of the Wellcome Trust and the National Archive, provides information on the location of hospital records in the United Kingdom. It is available on-line: www.nationalarchives.gov.uk/hospitalrecords/

Bethlem Royal Hospital Archives and Museum holds an extensive archive on Bethlem but also collections from several other asylums: www.bethlemheritage.org.uk

Index of English and Welsh Lunatic Asylums and Mental Hospitals www.mdx.ac.uk/WWW/STUDY/4_13_Ta.htm

The Summer Festival at the Royal Earlswood Idiot Asylum, Surrey, was a typical asylum fête. In this case, it was provided for the children who were treated and educated there. It included Punch and Judy, a band and a Fancy Fair in marquees. The public were admitted to see how well the children were treated. (*Illustrated London News*, 1867.)

PLACES TO VISIT

It is difficult to visit asylums. Most are no longer working hospitals. Many have been demolished. Others, even if they survive, are in private ownership, converted to residential apartments. Some asylums have their own museums of mental health, which provide excellent sources of material on the subject. Most have a website with further information on visiting.

Bethlem Royal Hospital Archives and Museum, Monks Orchard Road,
Beckenham, Kent. Telephone: 020 3228 4227.
Website: www.bethlemheritage.org.uk

Crichton Royal Hospital Museum, Crichton Royal Hospital, Easterbrook Hall,
Bankend Road, Dumfries. Telephone: 01387 267613.

Glenside Hospital Museum (Bristol Borough Asylum), University of the West
of England Glenside Campus, Stapleton, Bristol BS16 1DD.
Telephone: 0117 965 2688.
Website: www.glensidemuseum.pwp.blueyonder.co.uk

The Imperial War Museum, Lambeth Road, London SE1 6HZ. Telephone: 020
7416 5320. Website: www.iwm.org.uk
Housed in the third Bethlem building.

The Lightbox, Chobham Road, Woking, Surrey GU21 4AA.
Telephone: 01483 737800. Website: www.thelightbox.org.uk
Exhibitions on the history of mental health treatment including
asylums.

Science Museum, Exhibition Road, South Kensington, London SW7 2DD.
Telephone: 0870 870 4868. Website: www.sciencemuseum.org.uk
Medical exhibits.

Wellcome Library, Collection and Exhibitions, 183 Euston Road, London
NW1 2BE. Telephone: 020 7611 8722.
Website: http://library.wellcome.ac.uk

INDEX